SIERRA NEVADA

Facade of
14,375 foot (4382 meters)
Mount Williamson near
height of Mount Whitney
and 13,950 foot
(4352 meters) Trojan Peak
above rounded
desert granites
along Sierra
Nevada eastside.

SIERRA NEVADA

PHOTOGRAPHY BY DAVID MUENCH • TEXT DON PIKE

Dedicated
to all those
who share
in a continuing
appreciation
and preservation
of the range
of light—
patient and enduring
The Sierra Nevada.

International Standard Book Number 0-912856-49-1
Library of Congress Catalog Number 79-51769
Copyright© 1979 by Graphic Arts Center Publishing Co.
P.O. Box 10306 • Portland, Oregon 97210 • 503/224-7777
Designer • Bonnie Muench
Printer • Graphic Arts Center
Bindery • Lincoln & Allen
Printed in the United States of America
Second Printing

January escarpment
of the mighty
Sierra Nevada
at Big Pine faces
eastward to
ridges of the
Mohave Desert
above Owens Valley.
Palisades dominate
the crestline.

5

Sunrise on 12,944 foot
(3,945 meters) Lone Pine
Peak from the
Alabama Hills. Right:
The Sierra's highest
point of 14,496 foot
(4,418 meters) Mount Whitney
Pages 8 and 9: Sunrise
initiates exposure
of Mount Williamson.

Sierra Nevada crestline view
north from top of Mount Langley;
Sequoia National Park and the
John Muir Wilderness. Right:
Alabama Hills with 14,042 foot
(4,280 meters) Mount Langley.
Pages 12 and 13: Ridges of the
crestline north to Mount Darwin
from 14,162 foot (4,317 meters)
Mount Sill top, in Kings Canyon.

Yucca whipplei
in full May bloom
along roaring
South Fork of the
Kings river.
Left: Forested
ridges recede to
the west above the
South Fork, in Kings
Canyon National Park.

Rock narrows, South Fork
of the Kings River. Right:
Horseshoe Bend along South
Fork of the Kings River.
Detail: Blazing Star
Mentzelia laevicaulis.
Page 18: Oaks leafing out.
Page 19: Indian Paintbrush
against wall of metamorphosed
phyllite, Merced River Canyon.

Pages 20 and 21: California poppy
Eschscholtzia californica with
Bentham's lupine *Lupinus
benthamii,* western foothill country
in spring months.
Above: Dwarf monkey flower *Mimulus
nanus* in rock outcrop.
Left: Owls clover *Orthocarpus
purpurascens* and Ithuriel's spears
Brodiaea laxa in western foothills.

Pages 24 and 25: The
Merced River rushing and
leaping in wild exultation
over boulders of upper
Yosemite Valley.
Above: Vernal Falls
and Liberty Cap. Right:
Tamarack Creek
during a spring runoff,
Yosemite National Park.

Cathedral Rocks,
reflection in Merced
River overflow,
Yosemite Valley.
Right: Repeating forms
of Black oaks
and 2,565 foot
(782 meters) drop of
Yosemite Falls,
Yosemite National Park.

From Little Yosemite
Valley the Merced
River begins a leap of
597 feet (182 meters)
that is Nevada
Falls. Left: Yosemite
Valley. The glacial
sculptured walls
form the sheer brow
of Half Dome.

Turning leaves
of black oak
at foot of Sentinel
Rock in the Yosemite
Valley. Right: An
exuberant spray
of Cascade
Creek as it enters
Yosemite Valley over
a sheer granite wall.

32

Sun and shadow
accentuate patina
of glacial polish
on granite, in
Yosemite high country.
Left: A single
ponderosa needle in
moss coated glacial
erratic at the
foot of Royal Arches.

Storms' fury subsides
in gentle fog.
Clouds Rest
and glacial erratics
above Tenaya Canyon.
Detail: Upper
Yosemite Falls.
Right: Fog, sun
and Jeffery pine on
Sentinel Dome, Yosemite.

Half Dome and erratics,
brought down by
ancient glacier flow,
find a resting place
on granite rock
of Tenaya Canyon.
Right: Half Dome
reflection in late
summer flow of the
Merced River, Yosemite.

Blazing Star,
Mentzelia laevicaulis
and wild oats
in May profusion
along lower Tuolumne
River Canyon.
Left: Stonecrop
Cotyledon laxa blooms
on ancient rock facade,
Tuolumne River Canyon.

Fountainheads
high in the Sierras.
A slow June snowmelt
along Box Lake,
John Muir Wilderness.
Detail: Small pool on
John Muir Trail near
Ruby Lake. Right: Upper
Truckee River during
a spring snowstorm.

Dawn at Emerald Bay
and Lake Tahoe
from the California
side. Left: In Yosemite
National Park the
monolithic gate of
El Capitan and
Cathedral Rocks
reflect in the Merced
River at sunrise.

Winter moods of
Lake Tahoe.
Snow flurries
quietly curtain
Emerald Bay in
brooding stillness.
Left: Sunlight splinters
through cloud rifts
from Rose Knob
on the Nevada side.

Incense cedar and tall
bracken fern along
South Fork Kings River.
Detail: Five finger
ferns along Tallac Creek,
Desolation Wilderness.
Left: Spring flow of
Avalanche Creek
becomes Horsetail Falls
in Desolation Wilderness.

SIERRA NEVADA

Mountains are great teachers, and most youngsters who grew up running the ridges found out very early that the Sierra Nevada did not suffer fools gladly. The mountain world was not actively malevolent, at least not to one gang of unbridled hellions, but all of us learned that ignorance had to be tempered by caution, and stupidity was always suitably rewarded. The mountains taught us to look, and occasionally to see; they taught patience, endurance, courage of sundry types, and tolerance of a sort; and they showed us more about ourselves than we ever wanted, or bothered, to learn. In retrospect it would be easy to cast the mountains in the role of the stern father, firmly but lovingly bringing order and competence to otherwise unruly lives, but that mountain world was what it has always been—simply there, for man to make of it what he will.

We made a lot of mistakes, many of them corrected with lumps never wholly forgotten, but one of them the mountains never seemed to mind; we called them "the Sierras". It was an honest enough mistake, and remains a trifling distinction, but it once ignited a 20 minute trail-side lecture on the sanctity of "the Sierra" by a buffoon in leather shorts who dangled a peculiar tin cup from his belt. We decided he was a deranged beggar on an annual pilgrimage to his ground-squirrel guru. We would learn later that his ranks are legion, although the mountains never bothered to bury us in an avalanche for our heinous transgression.

Some years after I got the name right I learned from a similar oracle, this one wearing cordouroy shorts and boots that cost more than my truck, that I didn't even have the right mountains. I was informed, around a mouthful of compressed, high-protein tree bark, that the stream I was so diligently flogging with a dry fly was really not a Sierra brook. Brook? Rivers, streams, and creeks in the Sierra I had waded all my life, but no brook had ever dampened these sneakers; of course it was not a Sierra brook, it was a creek. That settled, it developed that this modest tributary of a branch of the north fork of the Feather River wasn't in the Sierra. Hmm . . . a southern arm of the Cascades perhaps? No, these bumps upon the land were not a part of the Sierra Nevada because they were not like the *real* Sierra to the south—the essential Sierra of granite polished to glistening smoothness, high altitude, vast roadless expanses above timberline, and redwood on the lower slopes.

While this revelation did not spawn immediate chagrin and confusion, it did open avenues for investigation, and over the intervening years it has become apparent that many writers, hikers, fishermen, photographers, climbers, campers, packers, and even geographers subscribe to this thesis in one degree or another. It really isn't important, I suppose, that some folks set the northern boundary of the Sierra at Sonora Pass, beautiful Lake Tahoe, or the Yuba River (the point varies in proportion to the logic behind it), but none have ever adequately explained what the mountains stretching northward to 10,457 foot (3181 meters) Lassen Peak are; after all, I may have expended a lot of years seriously lost.

This argument, seldom initiated but usually nourished by parochialism, elitism, ignorance, or boredom, is easy to understand. From Lassen Peak in the north to Tehachapie Pass in the south, the Sierra Nevada are extremely diverse, in composition, evaluation, altitude, and flora. These differences shaped man's history in the Sierra, and continues to affect how man lives, works, and plays in the mountains. Because of *how* they are, different regions shape man's perception of *what* they are, and sometimes, how they ought to be. Thus someone who has hiked the remote timberline of the southern range and learned to fondly embrace it may find little common ground with the gold country homeowner or the hunter on the lava ridges of the north. The tragedy is that in finding "the essential Sierra", some often completely overlook discovering the joy of the whole—no matter how dilute it may seem.

There are scores of demarcations for the Sierra Nevada, many amply justified for reasons of geography, geology, botany, or aesthetics. A concensus of the broader views could perhaps hold that there are generally three regions within the Sierra, distinct for all of those inherent reasons.

The rumpled reach of the Sierra north of Tahoe is the region most usually scorned by purists in pursuit of a definition. Here the mountains are lower, with peaks seldom reaching above 7,000 feet (2134 meters), a full 4,000 feet (1219 meters) lower than the high country further south. Consequently, the northern Sierra lack the familiar barren-ground vistas above timberline that characterize the southern mountains. Here, too, the land is characterized more by lava flows than glacially carved granite. Perhaps more importantly, the northern Sierra register the imprint of man's presence with roads, communities, industry, and grazing. This is a region where man can, has, and does live year-round, making the mountains his home, and turning the resources of the region into income. Almost a century of logging has veined these mountains with dirt roads, making nearly all of it readily accessible during the spring, summer, and fall. Communities that dot the range from eastern to western slope are tied together by all-weather roads, keeping the mountains alive with commerce through the winter. Although the northern Sierra are not cluttered with civilization, the continued presence of man has lent the region a distinctive ambiance. Essentially these are the accessible Sierra, and for some they can never be the genuine article.

If such a thing as the central Sierra could be said to exist, it would

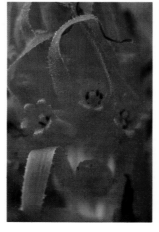

Early spring flowers on the snow plant. Right: Swelling force of the Merced River.

probably stretch from Donner Pass south to Sonora Pass. The American River provides a boundary of sorts, for south of it begins the readily apparent granite formations that characterize the southern mountains. The central region begins to blend the lava and granite that distinguish the extreme ends of the range. These mountains are cut by many roads also, including the major interstate ties across the Sierra, and during the last two decades many have been up-graded to all-weather status—a direct result of burgeoning winter sports activity. Population has also grown under the twin stimuli of accessibility and winter sports, creating a landscape and mood barely recognizable a quarter-century ago.

There exists a large body of opinion which insists that the Sierra really begin south of Sonora Pass, at the very least, that here is the essential Sierra, Muir's "Range of Light", which provides the distinctive qualities and majestic scenery that have made the Sierra famous. There is no argument that the southern mountains are distinctive and magnificent. Glacial sculpted granite, peaks that range from 11,000 to 14,000 feet (3353 to 4267 meters) in height, awesome big trees and alpine lakes scattered across a weather-beaten landscape above timberline all help to create an unforgettable mountain world. Here are the jagged peaks and granite escarpments that lured Clarence King and thousands of climbers after him to the Sierra Nevada. Here, too, are the vast reaches of roadless back-country, accessible only to the most determined, that prompt armies of acolytes to follow in Muir's footsteps. This is land as nature made it, both tempting and forbidding in a single encounter, at once atavistically powerful and delicately vulnerable. The high Sierra stirs fundamental passions in man, perhaps explaining in part the less than rational regionalism that often rears up to proclaim it the "essential Sierra."

The southern Sierra adds an extra dimension to its charm with the spectacular eastern escarpment. Lying in the rain shadow of the crest, the eastern slope is arid, sustaining largely desert plants and animals adapted to a dry environment. The effect of crossing the divide in the north and central Sierra can, with local exception, be very disappointing, but the jagged, rugged land of the south gives birth to an enchanting world. It is not wholly distinct in mood from the harsh land that soars above timberline on the western slope of the southern Sierra. This continuity may be what binds this reach of the mountains together, creating a compelling and memorable whole that seems greater than the sum of its parts.

Regardless of the differences that augur against unity, the Sierra Nevada has always been one range of mountains for me, and much of the attraction is the diversity that has spawned argument. They are not the same mountains from north to south, in mood, geology, or utility, and that is a wonderful thing. The Sierra can be a surpris-

ing, ever-changing experience—as they have been for generations of people—and to expect more, or less, of them is self-deluding. The Sierra have a multiplicity to offer, and have delivered an enormous quantity without question. They provided instruction, sustenance, income, recreation, and inspiration, but they never told one boy what to call them or pointed to where they ended. Maybe these mountains suffer some kinds of fools gently after all. Or perhaps they are simply patient with transients like man.

The Sierra was born roughly 130 million years ago during the Mesozoic era, when the earth wrinkled and bulged up out of the sea into high rolling hills. This rising surface masked the creation far beneath of a huge granite batholith, spawned out of molten rock, eventually solidifying into the granite masses so readily recognizable along the southern reaches of the range. For millions of years lush vegetation covered the old sea-bed, while wind and water began the erosion which gradually exposed the granite beneath, and began to cut ravines and ridges.

The volcanic turbulence which would remain an active part of the Sierra landscape to the present began about 20 million years ago, spreading massively deep flows of lava across the northern end of the range. As recently as two million years ago, volcanic activity was initiating dramatic changes in the landscape near Lassen Peak, creating Brokeoff, Red Mountain, and Prospect Peak. Through this era of vulcanism, the range was still experiencing uplift, although the most dramatic change came late.

The Sierran uplift was the result of a block fault, a massive fracture along the eastern edge of the range and the subsequent tilting of the mass, rising most quickly in the east and sloping gently away to the west. Over 125 million years the successive lifts had raised the mountains to seven or eight thousand feet above the sea, but about four or five million years ago a shattering burst of activity pushed the block up an additional 6,000 feet (1829 meters), to its present height. This great upheaval lifted the land that would become the Central Valley, and pushed up the Coast Range. The ocean withdrew from beaches along the Sierra to regroup along the Coast Range, and the stage was set for the next great era of mountain sculpting.

Although this last great lift had created the mass of the Sierra, they would have been unrecognizable to most 20th century enthusiasts. Much of the distinctive mountain profile is due to four successive ice movements during the last million years; glaciation that was a direct result of that last massive tilting and uplift. The ice which carved the Sierra during the Pleistocene epoch was not a part of the continental sheets which ground their way across most of the rest of North America, but rather were of local origin. The Sierra, which before the final tilt had pushed clouds riding the prevailing westerlies off

the Pacific high enough to precipitate rain, now could push them higher still, to create snow. During the four intervals of global cooling that created the ice ages, snow was dumped on the Sierra faster than summer thaw could remove it. Huge drifts formed gradually pushing a crushing weight of compacted snow and ice down slope, and glaciation had begun.

At the peak of glaciation, the ice floes stretched for 300 miles along the divide, at times reaching 60 miles toward the valley. There is evidence to infer that in heaviest concentration, some glaciers were a mile thick. These rumbling, gnashing, engines of excavation, moving simply because their enormous mass sought a place of rest, scraped up and gouged out all but the highest peaks in the range and did more to shape the mountains we know than any other one agency.

As the great rivers of ice ground their way down the mountains they smoothed the edges on ravines, turning the V-shaped valleys carved by rivers and streams into flatter floored U-shaped valleys like Kings Canyon and Yosemite Valley, filing off smaller buttresses, straightening twisted streambeds, and leaving the hardest formations to be exposed upon withdrawal. From the glacial calving-grounds near the peaks where infant flows hollowed out the cirques, to lower ridges completely over-ridden by mature glaciers, the ice carved stunning jagged pinnacles and sharp, ragged ridges.

In the course of their passage the glaciers vacuumed up loose sand, rocks, and any other debris not immovably anchored, using it as an abrasive along the way, and depositing the remains along the sides and leading edges of the glaciers as they withdrew. These small ridges, or moraines, though liberally scattered across the mountain landscape, are eroded or overgrown into anonymity, but the effect of their presence is obvious. Many of the small mountain lakes are the result of terminal moraines that impound the annual run-off; others formed lakes that gradually filled with sediment, to become mountain meadows. The meadows on the floor of Yosemite were the result of just such a process. Lateral moraines have left gravel embankments across otherwise virgin wilderness that look almost engineered, as though some transportation department road-bed crew had run amok; occasionally melting glaciers dropped boulders large and small across bald granite terraces, like marbles on some giant abandoned playground.

The last major glacial activity in the Sierra receded some 10,000 to 20,000 years ago, but small vestigial remains still lurk in sun-shaded cirques. Some estimates put the current number at about 50, a 60 percent reduction from the number at the time of Clarence King's mountain survey, and most are more rock and debris than ice, pale reminders of the great frozen rivers that shaped so much of the Sierra that we now know.

Today the most powerful engine of change in the mountains following man, is the weather, most specifically the winter weather. Lichen may nibble chemically at rock, the random root will fracture granite, and summer winds may move dust and soften a jagged edge, but winter's moisture in its various forms is now the big mover and shaker in the mountains. Rain finds its way into tiny cracks and fissures, there to freeze and expand, cracking and faulting the rock usually on a small scale, but occasionally fracturing loose gigantic slabs from granite domes. Now pockets form on the rock, collecting wind-borne soil, and eventually trapping a seed that raises a new plant with tunneling roots. The Sierra' face begins to change. Through the winter, avalanches can gouge the face of slopes and fill ravines with jumbled wreckage, but the most consistent, inexorable activity comes in the spring, during the thaw and runoff. From tiny rivulets barely able to tumble sand to raging floods that topple trees and smash buildings, water finding its way downhill works to define and reduce the Sierra. Gullies are deepened, top-soil is stripped from unprotected hillsides, plants large and small are displaced, animals may move to keep up with a shifting food chain, and meadows are created in the alluvial fan of seasonal washes. Every year the Sierra is changed by the water of winter, sometimes only minutely to the perceptions of man, but in the less transient scope of geologic time the mountains are being steadily worn down.

The Sierra Nevada is the great arbiter of weather for itself and the entire state it borders. The foundation of California's fantastic wealth is the intensive agriculture practiced on the floor of the San Joaquin and Sacramento Valleys, and the agriculture is made possible by warm winter rains and mountain run-off collected for the summer; both are a product of the Sierra. The prevailing westerlies that course across the Pacific toward the continent soak up moisture from the ocean, and this air manages to retain most of its vapor despite minor obstacles like the Coast Range. The gentle rise of the western slope of the Sierra, however, forces that air higher, cooling it, and forcing the vapor to precipitate as rain and snow. During the winter, when the high pressure moves offshore, the jet-stream flattens out, and the winds have a straight shot at the coast, the air mass piling against the mountains yields rain on the valley floor. More falls on the foothills, running into reservoirs to begin the collection process that will be completed when the heavy snow accumulation melts in the late spring and early days of summer.

At higher, cooler, altitudes the moisture condenses as snow, and as early as November the snow pack that will eventually pile to depths of 50 and 60 feet can begin to develop, and will continue to collect through March. Storms can strike in October and linger until May or June, but the preponderance of snow collects from December

Dogwood blooms along the Merced River in Yosemite Valley. Right: Moss on tree trunk.

through early March. At lower elevations few storms in the Sierra are howling blizzards of drifting, man-killing snow, but around the higher peaks, especially in the southern end, winds whip up to 80 and 100 miles an hour. Winter does not exclude man from the mountains, and in the northern and central Sierra play displaces work in what seems to be almost equal intensity. Caution must be exercised, but life, work, and recreation continue under skies that are clear as often as they are cloudy.

Spring is elusive in the Sierra because altitude and latitude vary so widely. Grasses along the lower foothills of the northern range can be turning a crispy brown in mid-June, when snow is just beginning to melt off the seed-bed of alpine flowers in the high southern peaks. Cold nights near the peaks can hold back spring for a month or more after daytime temperatures have become a convincing argument that summer has arrived, with some higher altitudes showing only 60 frost free days a year. Despite a symbolic heritage as a time or rebirth and renewed vigor, over the short haul the spring thaw can create more obstacles to activity than it eliminates: torrential creeks close normally shallow fords, once frozen roads become bottomless bogs, and forests easily crossed on skis become slippery, soggy nightmares for foot travel. Because spring is not sudden and universal, the signs have to be closely watched, ere you join the rest of us amid a springtime bouquet of knee-deep mud. The woods are charming and the mountains romantic; reality lurks in the goo.

The mountains were created by monumental forces within and without, and the mountains in turn contributed largely to the weather that surrounds them, but for many of us their real fascination lies in the plant and animal life, that the mountains and the weather combine to create and sustain. Because diversity is the long suit in the Sierra, generalizations are often futile and always fraught with exceptions; the kind reader is herewith forewarned that this writer has picked the cranial cavities both scholarly and practical for many years, has looked at and lived with these mountains for a quarter century, and still doesn't believe all his own conclusions. Therein, perhaps, explains much of the enchantment of these mountains. A case in point might be illustrative.

As a young boy, I often came in contact with a dirt road that generally meandered north and south along the foothills. Not only were north-south roads rare in my part of the mountains (most adopted a no-nonsense approach straight up ridges or ravines to the heart of the mountains), but this one had signs that hinted at origins in some long abandoned Works Progress Administration project which proclaimed it Ponderosa Way. From a broad, graded, graveled road it would disappear entirely, re-emerging as a cat-track; it crossed creeks on engineered concrete bridges and logs spiked together; and

it managed to avoid being recorded on about half the maps extant. It was a real puzzle for young folks, and, as it turned out, for grownups, too; when I finally screwed up the courage to reveal rampaging ignorance, nobody seemed to know the why or wherefore of Ponderosa Way. It took many years, and a city bred colleague with a penchant for arcane detail, to learn that Ponderosa Way was originally intended not only as an access road for logging and fire protection, but also as a line of demarcation running the length of the Sierra, separating the mountains proper from the foothills. More specifically, the idea was to trace the lower limit of the pine belt, scribing a line above the scrub oak and digger pine of the foothill country. Anyone who has ever followed portions of the road knows that although the idea may be absolutely sound, the Sierra failed to cooperate. Life zones trickle back and forth so casually, and micro-environments create pockets of unlikely vegetation so readily, that any single line would bend into a corkscrew, and tangents, hooks, and spurs would decorate its entire length. I *never* would have guessed the theory behind Ponderosa Way from watching the vegetation, and, nursing a wounded vanity all the while, doubt seriously that anyone else would either.

Granting a degree of flexibility there are four—some insist five as the minimum consideration—life zones in the Sierra. All reach greater altitude in the south than the north, and some marked changes occur, but in general there is the foothill country, the ponderosa forests, the red fir-lodgepole belt, and the Alpine Zone. Convincing arguments can be made for further subdivision—especially for the inclusion of a Sub-Alpine Zone—but this is the way one gang of rowdies learned to recognize the gib woods, and it stuck.

The foothills of the Sierra, generally characterized by the lowly digger pine and scattered scrub oak, seldom generate a lot of enthusiasm among mountaineers. Ranging in altitude from 3,000 feet (914 meters) in the north to 5,000 feet (1524 meters) in the south, the region seldom inspires superlatives, but it is the wintering ground of many grazing and predatory animals, from deer to coyotes and mountain lions. The native grasses and browse of the chaparral provide feed for some, and the predators follow by necessity. Its streams are often choked by willows and in summer much of it turns the dirty brown of dry grass, but nearly year-round accessibility makes it the main-traveled road for many.

The ponderosa, or yellow pine, belt begins where the foothill diggers and oaks end and extends to 5,000 or 6,000 feet in the north and up to 9,000 feet (2743 meters) in the south. The ponderosa forest is also populated by sugar pines, Douglas fir, white fir, and cedars, which make this the most attractive region for those seeking marketable timber. It also makes the forest very attractive and pleas-

ant for visitors. Summertime temperatures are generally mild, and where virgin pine duff still exists the walking is easy and vistas pleasant. For the most part, the forest is not impenetrably dense, animals from rodents to deer as well as songbirds and hawks provide abundant diversion, and many hikers not smitten by the alpine lorelei regard this as the archetypal forest.

The ponderosa belt suffers only one serious drawback, aside from the overpopulation that besets the entire range, and that is a plant rather decorously known as manzanita which manifests itself wherever a foothold is granted. Any open scar, from an old burn to a clearcut, is quickly overgrown with manzanita, often to depths of six or eight feet. We always called it buckbrush, because deer were the only critters bigger than a ring-tailed civit cat that could get through it, and because the biggest bucks always spent the fall lurking within, while young nimrods grumbled without. There are six varieties of manzanita extant in the Sierra, all with individual names, but those monikers bear no resemblance to the names applied by anyone caught in the stuff. Usually this happens because it looks like a short-cut, and the vegetation seems dense enough to support someone walking carefully on top. So much for short-cuts and appearances. Manzanita blights the Sierra from one end to the other, and seriously hampers most re-forestation projects, but small critters love the food supply and sanctuary it provides.

There is an entirely new dimension added to the ponderosa belt in the southern Sierra, for it is here that the big trees grow, Sequoia gigantea, the Sierra redwood. These massive trees, some reaching 35 feet thick and 300 feet high, are the biggest trees in the world and are formed nowhere but in the Sierra. Were it not for the withered bristlecone pine which clings grimly to the rocks above timberline, the sequoia would be the oldest living plant as well. The redwood of the Sierra is related to the more numerous coast redwood, Sequoia sempervirius, but it is far bigger. They are so huge that they could be grotesque, dwarfing as they do the surrounding trees, but the redwoods are saved by a grace and balance that leaves mortal architects mumbling. John Muir raved at length on the subject of the "Big Trees" as he called them, waxing eloquent and profound in descriptive narrative; after one look at these trees, Muir's prose pales into insignificance. So does everyone else's.

Without question, the Sierra redwood is a tough and tenacious organism, a fact which made it possible for some to survive 4,000 years of fire, lightning, and insects. The forest fires which periodically swept the Sierra were seldom able to destroy mature sequoia because the thick bark contains no resins or saps, and insulates the body of the trees from the heat. The bark also protects the trees from the devastating effects of lightning strikes. Being a redwood, the sequoia is marvelously resistant to disease and decay, and unpalatable to insects. Apparently the most vulnerable portion of these big trees is the root system, which is shallow; many wind fall trees are thought to have been vigorous, healthy specimens when they toppled.

Probably the Sierra redwoods' biggest enemy is the hand of man, who cut a wide swath while making every effort to exploit the redwoods for timber and tourism. Fortunately the sequoia makes lousy lumber compared to its hapless relative the coast redwood and the trees often shatter on impact when fallen. Although many were cut for fence posts before the turn of the century, it wasn't difficult to persuade the logging industry to concentrate on the pines and firs, and today virtually all that remain are preserved in some 36,000 acres of carefully protected groves. During the latter half of the 19th century and into the 20th, many were cut, carved, and hollowed into dance floors, drive-through trees, and multi-room houses as curiosities to stimulate the mushrooming tourist industries. Most such antics proved fatal to the trees.

Today, in stands protected from harvest and nonsense, the sequoia are the lodestones of some of the Sierra's most beautiful forests. Unlike the coast redwood, which grows like an exclusive club, seldom permitting lesser trees to share the same ground, the democratic Sierra redwood grows in perfect harmony with pines, firs, and cedars. The range of the redwood is limited, however, to the southern portion of the Sierra.

Above the immensely valuable pinery, is the red fir-lodgepole belt, which runs right over the crest in the north, and climbs to 10,000 feet in the south. Although the fir and lodgepole do not co-mingle extensively, they both tend to grow in dense groves, creating a similar mood in the forest. The woods are dark, littered with deadfall and debris, and generally so tangled that walking through is as often a chore as it is a pleasure. I have always enjoyed these forests, not only for the mysterious mood which pervades them, but also for the abundant animal life they support. Almost all critters like a place to hide, and lots of obstacles for pursuers, and the fir-lodgepole regions provide such an environment. Here experience and common-sense in navigating the forest are taxed to their utmost, but the rewards are also the greatest.

These altitudes are also the most common region for aspen, and one of the Sierra's ineffable delights is to break out of a lodgepole tangle into a broad meadow accented by "quakers". If there is a heaven, it has to be a summer meadow freshened by an afternoon down-slope breeze stirring the aspen. Although they teem with life, much of it delicate and vulnerable, some of it brutal, all of it in a constant state of change, these mountain meadows bespeak a tranquility that can be found nowhere else.

Eastern flank of Sierra Nevada. Right: Reflection of Mount Solomons into Helen Lake.

In contrast to the darkling close quarters and soft contours of the fir and lodgepole forests, movement upward into the alpine zone telescopes life into abrupt lines and harsh edges. It is an uncompromising land above timberline, where a few lodgepoles and juniper pines struggle up to 11,000 feet before they give up, to be replaced by the even hardier foxtail pines, a cousin to the bristlecone. It is a life zone almost completely unique to the southern end of the range, for the northern mountains simply do not reach high enough. This is the region that sends enthusiasts tumbling into hyperbole, providing most of the ammunition for arguments which proclaim the southern mountains "the essential Sierra."

The alpine regions are a curious admixture of the large and the small: huge mountains, high altitude, or long vistas provide the backdrop for a world of plants scaled in miniature. Low moisture, brutal winds, shallow soils, and a short growing season keep flowers; trees, brush, and grasses small, and many seem to huddle close to the ground for protection. The 60-day growing season dictates in large measure what may grow here, but hardiness and tenacity may play as large a role. High winds keep many ridges and hillsides snow-free during the winter, removing the protection of drifted snow from sedges, trees, and brush. During summer you will find these plants grimly clutching a small patch of soil between the rocks, gallantly pushing forth new growth.

At lower alpine levels, meadows provide the food supply for mice and chipmunks, who in turn attract badgers, foxes, coyotes, hawks, eagles and other predators. Deer often wend their way up to this elevation for short periods of time, but retreat into the protection of the lower forests, usually before the first indication of storms. The truly high country is the preserve of determinedly elusive animals like the bighorn sheep, and the particularly well adapted pika, who doesn't hibernate, but cuts his hay, and cures it in the sun before storing it carefully for the winter.

It is a land stripped of the superfluous, dominated by bare granite and the wind. Seasonal life can and does soften the aspect, but here, more than anywhere else in the Sierra, man must recognize himself as an intruder and interloper—and a temporary one at that.

There is another side to the Sierra, one most strikingly seen along the eastern slope of the southern mountains. Lying in the rain shadow of the crest, is desert country, a land sometimes not too different in aspect from the alpine zones. In the north this dry country is less spectacular, but in the south the abrupt shattering along the tilting fault block created 3,000 feet of crags and cliffs that provides both definition and backdrop. Although the juniper, jeffrey, lodgepole and even aspen that inhabit the western slope find their way across the crest to the eastern scarp, the co-mingling with desert adapted

sagebrush and piñon cast a different mood. There is seldom any doubt that this is the fringe of the desert, and even late snow trapped in high cirques does little to dispel that knowledge. This high desert country can be spell-binding for some, trapping their spirits so completely that they never leave, content to scratch out a living where nature takes the maximum measure of each and every individual. It is not an easy land to live with, and sometimes even to visit, but somehow it always seems to give more to the spirit than it takes from the body…well, almost always.

It would be simplistic to suggest that the incredible variety of the Sierra offers something for everyone, because it doesn't. These mountains provide an arena for imagination, determination, wit, strength, courage, testing, reflection, and growth, but men who would use it must bring more than just a body and intellect in repose. Nothing will happen for an organism or mind in stasis, except perhaps that moss will grow on it.

Of the men who came to the Sierra, probably none understood it better, took less, gave more, and left fewer marks of his passage than the Indians. Estimates of the Indian population of the Sierra, of the tribal members who actually lived in the mountains or drew the majority of their sustenance from them, range as high as a quarter of a million. Given the overall Amerind population of the 18th century, 15 to 20 percent of America's Indians lived in the Sierra. By aboriginal standards that is high density, and speaks clearly for the region's ability to sustain life.

Unlike the Indians of the high plains and Rockies, they were not a warrior society, where the measure of a man's worth was taken in combat or larceny. They were a singularly peaceful and gentle people, so much so, in fact, that many whites conditioned by nomadic plains warriors regarded them as slow-witted and contemptible. They were, in general, hunters and gatherers who traded extensively with their neighbors, but who preferred to keep their small bands and extended families in their home territories. They seem to have been extremely well satisfied with their lot, content to adjust their lives to the changing seasons and the sudden vicissitudes of nature, earning a rather comfortable living from the mountains for themselves and their families.

Anthropological classification of Indians by whatever method usually degenerates into a maze of detail or a muddle of sweeping generalization. While the former may be more accurate, it is usually hopelessly confusing; the latter is much easier to fully understand, inspires great confidence, and inevitably generates a forest of footnotes to catalogue the exceptions. Normally it is preferable to avoid both approaches, but that contributes nothing to understanding, induces nervous tension and apoplexy in publishers, and generates,

nasty, spiteful letters from anthropologists. What follows is a compromise, with apologies to truth.

Among the Indians of the Sierra there were five basic language groups: the Maidu, Miwok, Yokut, Mono, and Washoe. The Maidu lived in the foothills north and south of the Feather River country, where mild winters made it possible for many of them to live year-round in the mountains. North of the Maidu were the Yana, who lived in the Mill and Deer Creek drainages, lived a life very similar to the Maidu, but must be classed linguistically with the Washo, who inhabited the eastern slope. South of the Maidu lived the Miwok, who covered the foothills and valley south from the American River. The Yokut occupied the southern end of the Sierra, from roughly the Fresno River southward. Their opposite number on the east side of the mountains were the Mono, who generally regarded everything from Owens Valley and Mono Lake to the high Sierra as home. North of them, in the Carson and Truckee country, the Washo lived along the eastern slope.

These large groupings can be very misleading, for although the small bands within a language group were seldom actively hostile to one another, there was little solidarity, harmony, or communication (other than that necessitated by trade) between the bands. Not only did they seldom co-operate, many times it was well nigh impossible for them to even understand their neighbors in the adjoining drainage. This insularity was possible because there were few external threats that co-operation could overcome and there was plenty to eat, so pooling of resources or labor was not necessary. On the whole, life for the Indians of the Sierra was easy, although the Washo and Mono found they had to scramble a little harder than the residents of the western slope. Food was plentiful in the form of nuts, berries, acorns, fish, and large and small game. The climate was mild, and seasonal extremes could be avoided by moving up-slope in the summer and down to the valley floor in the winter. It was a pleasant, uncomplicated way of life, and the mountains demanded little for the bounty they provided, but this idyllic existence was shattered by the coming of the white man.

The Spanish, and subsequent Mexican, dominance over California had surprisingly little impact upon the Sierra Indians, for the simple reason that the Spanish had little interest in them. Occasionally a mountain Indian would be carted off to a mission for conversion and salvation, ultimately to repay the debt thus incurred by hard labor in the fields, but normally contact was limited to hiding a runaway valley or coastal Indian from the friars' press gangs. The real difficulty began with the appearance of Americans chasing the prospect of gold into the heart of the mountains. Rudely displaced when they presumably formed a barrier, actively hunted for sport and

revenge, and indifferently despoiled by disease and starvation, the ever so gentle Indians of the Sierra were no competition for the technological juggernaut of American civilization on the make. By the early 20th century the Indian population had been reduced to ten percent of the number extant when the Spanish arrived. Mourning their passing and the destruction of their way of life is as futile as keening over mountains that are no longer what they once were—but it comes naturally just the same.

The Spanish showed little interest in the Sierra Indians because they had little interest in the Sierra themselves. Although it was a Spanish missionary, Fray Pedro Font, looking east from the Sacramento-San Joaquin delta country who first spied its gleaming peaks and named it *"una gran sierra nevada"* (a great snowy range). They were more preoccupied with building a civilization along the coast and in the more fertile inland valleys. There was more than enough to keep them busy elsewhere, and the *sierra nevada* presented a forbidding, unprofitable aspect.

Unlike the Spaniards who chose to avoid any contact with the Sierra Nevada simply by ignoring them, Americans intent on crossing the continent could not avoid them, and eventually would actively seek them out. The first recorded crossing of the Sierra was made by an American, Jedediah Smith; strangely enough, the crossing was from west to east. Smith was a literate, religious, judicious mountain man—which may be a contradiction in terms—who came to California across the Mojave in 1826 to evaluate the beaver prospects. After being summarily ordered out by Mexican authorities, Smith and his party ignored the instructions and headed north along the foothills. The beaver were unpromising, but when Smith probed into the mountains in search of a way home, once along the Kings River and again at the American, he found the Mountains choked with snow. After wintering over on the Stanislaus River, Smith struck out in May of 1827, and eventually struggled over the crest somewhere near Ebbetts Pass.

In 1833 Joseph Reddeford Walker made the first crossing from east to west, in October, over a route so difficult no road or trail follows it today. The most notable aspect of the trek, apart from Walker's survival, was the first sighting of Yosemite by a white man. Zenas Leonard, the chronicler of the odyssey, marveled at the view, but the party trudged on without further investigation, seeking instead the sanctuary of the central valley beyond. The following year Walker would return to the states by a more salubrious southern route, crossing the pass which still bears his name.

The climate and fertility of California's great inland valley beckoned strongly during the 1840's, and in 1841 the Bartleson-Bidwell immigrant party abandoned their wagons in the face of the formid-

Ice-snow forms on top of Mount Langley. Right: View to the south from Mount Sill top.

able mountains, and made an October crossing somewhere near Sonora Pass. They were fortunate that the early winter in the high country was mild that year, and the group emerged relatively unscathed down the Stanislaus drainage. In 1845 the Stephans party struggled over the Sierra near Donner Pass with incredible difficulty, dismantling their wagons and hauling them piecemeal over the crest. Part of the group was forced to winter in the deep snows before pushing on in the spring, but they did so without loss of life—in fact, a child was born during the ordeal. The Stephans party, despite the difficulties and delays, became the first group to cross with wagons. Later that same year William B. Ide, who would become California's first and only President during the brief Republic, improved the Donner grade enough to make passage possible without dismantling the wagons. In 1846 the Donner party achieved a grisly sort of notoriety through a combination of poor judgment and bad luck—poor judgment in trying the mountains at the end of October, and bad luck in that the winter was more severe than it had been for the Stephans party. Forty people perished for the rest of us to learn that the Sierra can be brutal, uncompromising country.

The Sierra as an obstacle was being gradually eroded, but the gold rush in 1848 hastened the process abruptly. From the time of James Marshall's discovery in January, a flood of humanity began pouring over the mountains. Jim Beckwourth found a pass in the north that became the route of the Marysville Road; the legendary Kit Carson, who had accompanied Fremont's ineffectual fumblings through the mountains in 1844, found a poor if passable route south of Tahoe through a pass which still bears his name. The Carson trace carried much of the traffic over the mountains for nearly a decade until John Johnson pioneered a trail over Echo Summit that would become the Placerville Road, and later Highway 50.

By 1868 the last of the major trans-Sierra routes were opened when Theodore Judah surveyed the line for the Central Pacific Railroad, reviving and improving the Stephans trail over Donner Pass. The mountains that had once been a formidable barrier were now proving more tractable, and the Sierra—so long ignored by the Spanish, and first regarded by Americans as a troublesome obstacle to be overcome, had become an object of intense interest. These mountains, were the source of abundant wealth, just waiting for men of vision, daring, and greed to exploit.

Man's encroachment on the mountains has brought change, often catastrophic change that is easy to deplore and difficult or impossible to repair. Some of the devastation was unnecessary, some was due to lack of foresight, and some could have been mended by timely modification of methods. Much of the surgery that man practiced on the face of the Sierra was an inevitable by-product of tapping the

range's wealth, and unless we are willing to forsake all that such wealth contributed to the West's growth, and all that these mountains contribute to our present comfortable and secure life, we must be willing to accept the fact of change. Compromise in the face of burgeoning population and diminishing resources is not easy, and sacrifice of some kind must be made; the choices are not easy and are not softened by self-justifying platitudes, but that is man's burden in measuring his responsibility to himself, his species, and his land.

When we just began to exploit the resources of the Sierra there was little breast beating and anguished navel-gazing—the bounty seemed limitless and the excitement of wealth and the 19th century demigod Progress pushed all such considerations aside. Sierra Nevada gold provided the money, population, and commercial enterprise that would make California the leading state in the west, and keep her there. They were exciting times.

When James Marshall found a trace of gold in a tailrace at Sutter's Colona mill in 1848, he touched off a mining industry that would take two and one half billion dollars out of the Sierra Nevada over the next century. The first argonauts during the rush of '49 fit the popular image of grizzled sourdoughs scampering over the ridges and huddling by a stream, swirling sand in a pan. But the easily accessible placer gold quickly gave out and the miners formed companies, or were hired by entrepreneurs, to dam and divert whole streams to get at the gravel in the bed. Flumes were constructed to carry water to dry diggings, and the miners began to leave an altered landscape behind along with their trash. In three short years they took out a quarter of a billion dollars worth of gold, and that was only the beginning.

As the placer gold diminished, men began to attack the gold locked in the mountains. Hydraulic mining, where giant monitors aimed jets of water at the hillsides, was the first response. The mud washed down was run over riffle boxes where the gold was trapped, and the slurry discharged into creeks and rivers. The method was reasonably efficient, though expensive, and grossed another quarter billion dollars for the state's mining industry. Hydraulic mining also massacred the landscape, creating enormous scars like Malakoff diggings that will never recover, and silting the streams and rivers of the great valley until winter flooding became an annual festivity. Interestingly, it was the silting that brought legislation to stop hydraulic mining in 1884, and not concern over the indelible marks that designate destruction of the Sierra. Hard rock mining, where the veins of gold were pursued deep into the mountains, produced most of the gold taken from the Sierra, and did far less permanent damage than hydraulic efforts. But the advent of deep shaft hard rock mining had another, more visible, effect; those great holes in the earth consumed a dense forest of trees for timbering and fuel.

The Sierra forests were initially exploited to feed the mining industry, providing wood for sluices, flumes, and timbers. Because transportation was difficult from the Sierra pineries to the valley and coast towns, most of the lumber used by flat-landers during California's first decade came from coastal forests. Not until almost 1870, when the Central Pacific (the predecessor of the Southern Pacific) could provide rail shipment of logs throughout the valley, did the Sierra produce for more than local use. That use was, however, prodigal; the Comstock lode fueled with a fever of speculation consumed virtually all the timber from the Tahoe basin, and hydraulic and hard rock operations worked very hard at denuding the mother lode country.

The use of this timber need not have been a disaster, but the supply seemed inexhaustible and men grew careless. Clear-cutting—the practice of stripping every tree from a block of forest—was the normal method of harvest, which left hillsides unprotected from erosion. The less marketable timber was cut and left as slash, which was not only ugly, but left no trees to shade and protect seedlings. Brush found the environment attractive, though, and slopes which could have been nurturing valuable second growth timber raised only tangled thickets of buckbrush.

The state moved to encourage less wasteful and destructive practices in 1883 with the State Board of Forestry, to be joined by the federal government in 1905, when the Forest Service was founded. Regulation and a semblance of management helped to reduce the excesses, and improvements in harvesting and reforestation methods—often instituted by lumber companies themselves—have brought continual improvement to Sierra forests. The problems are by no means solved, for logging is a messy, destructive business, but too many people demand the necessities, comforts, and conveniences in the form of lumber, pulp, and packaging that come out of the mountains to suddenly stop harvesting the trees. Logging scars virgin forest, forever altering the primeval aspect that once reigned, and yet for all of us who grew up with these mountains it is a way of life, almost the natural order of things. Done sensibly, and with even a modicum of respect for the land, the forests of the Sierra can help to make our lives better indefinitely. We must be practical; just try to return as much as we take.

Stockmen have also harvested the Sierra, beginning as early as 1870 and continuing to today. Like the miners and loggers, the stockmen were careless, lulled by the seemingly endless supply of grass that grew each spring from the foothills to the high meadows. Overgrazing is not an uncommon practice in newly opened pastoral territories, for each is different and experience is the only reliable index. Overgrazing invariably leads to erosion, the extinction of some grasses and occasional permanent damage to delicate meadowlands. The Sierra grasslands were badly damaged by too much pressure, especially in the southern end of the range, and although strict regulation today prevents any recurrence, the quickest way to induce frothing paranoia in a preservationist is to suggest sheep grazing in the high mountains. John Muir, who saw the worst of the damage first-hand, dubbed them "hooved locust", an appelation which has such a wonderful ring to it that it is gleefully resurrected, often by people ill-qualified to judge either cause or effect. Curiously enough, state and federal foresters have begun to assess the damage of "over-tramping", if you will, by what might be termed "vibram-soled locust." The effect in many micro-environments is apparently considerable and devastating.

Probably the greatest resource the Sierra provides is water, a contribution which continues to grow more critical every year. The Sierra traps and stores most of California's fresh water in the snow-pack, releasing it through the spring and early summer melts. The trouble develops because the snow melts too quickly, and man must intercede to help the storage process with dams and reservoirs. Flood control also entered the picture very early, subsequently to be joined by electrical generation. The problem first reached large-scale proportions in 1913 when Los Angeles, stymied from further anticipated growth by a lack of water, legally stole the water of the Owens Valley and aquaducted it away. Stoutly buttressed arguments are advanced that this project benefitted a greater number of people and contributed more to the state's wealth than the continued health of the Owens Valley agricultural industry ever could, but people were already beginning to pause and wonder if the rewards justified the sacrifice. Hindsight and the megalopolis south of the Tehachapis renders a moot question in the minds of some.

The parameters of the debate which rages most vociferously today were first delineated in 1934, when the Hetch Hetchy canyon was dammed to supply reliable water for San Francisco. As this beautiful gorge, remembered now only in photographs that depict scenery as enchanting as Yosemite's, disappeared forever beneath the rising water people began to question the wisdom of these engineering marvels. Arguments which pit intangibles like beauty, wilderness, and future generations against bitter realities like growing population, thirsty cities and industries, and future generations are difficult to evaluate and balance. Too often the decision boils down to whose ox is being gored, and who has the motivating power to make their desires prevail. Who knows, perhaps divine providence has dictated that is the approach to the way it should be. The Sierra spent 120 million years changing the way it looked and functioned. Yes, man

may have accelerated that process and perhaps, to his own detriment.

Water projects have proliferated in direct proportion to the state's seemingly endless insatiable need for water. Folsom, Friant, Auburn, and Oroville dams are all parts of that massive growth, with many smaller reservoirs maintained for power supply, flood control, and water supply dotting the Sierra landscape. While many have clogged small canyons and tamed wild streams, they provide a different tempo of recreation to visitors in addition to the direct economic returns. The question is difficult to resolve, fraught with compromises that appear to satisfy no one, and rancorous beyond belief. The struggle over the future of the Stanislaus River was fought with a life-and-death intensity, as though more were at stake than white water, trees, dirt, and rock; perhaps there was.

The question is so confusing to me because the example closest to my experience still breeds ambivalent feelings. I grew up with the Feather River, once regarded as the West's premier trout stream and sculptor of some stunning canyon wilderness. Pacific Gas and Electric Company began the hydroelectric development of the North Fork before my time, taming that stretch of wild river before I could ever experience it. Although I probably should, I feel no bitterness because that canyon is still a charming place. The river still runs between the generating plants, albeit more slowly and warmer which discourages trout and encourages junk fish, but the fishing is decent and the bald eagles on the ridges are exciting. The power plants are examples of organic architecture at its best, as many seem to grow out of the canyon walls; the efficiency of using the water again and again through successive generators down the canyon stirs fundamental emotions in my Scotch soul. Without question the small plants are preferable to one massive impound of water, and perhaps because I grew up with it the whole conglomeration seems to fit. I don't feel offended by the end result, and even the river seems comfortable with the compromise. Unquestionably, many of us enjoy the benefits of the power thus generated. Even were the North Fork suddenly returned to its wild state, it probably would not be a very pleasant place; the easy access would encourage rampaging hordes of hikers, campers, and sundry other transients.

The construction of Oroville Dam lower down on the Feather still raises laments over the inundation of this portion of the river, but once again ambivalence rears its ugly head. I don't like reservoirs on general principles, and for most of the conventional reasons (although I would use the water and power dispensed by the facility with a greed matching anyone's), but I am not overwhelmed in throes of grief for the land lost. With very minor exception, those canyons were not pretty, not unique, and not inviting. If a positive benefit results, which it has, I can live with the dam. For any who regret the passing of the wild Feather River, there is still the Middle Fork, forever preserved in its natural state. It is stunningly beautiful and primitive country, that beggars description and successfully discourages all but the most determined visitors.

I love wild country, and find great comfort in mountain solitude. The imprint of man upon the Sierra offends more often than not, and my emotions resent man's technological inroads, but the outrage is tempered by the wavering knowledge that we must use and enjoy these mountains. It is easy to argue that the Sierra can be used without being destroyed, but destruction is a deceptive phantom. Yosemite, the incomparable valley, is well protected from exploitation by industry, and still boasts the geography and flora that flooded the senses a century ago, and yet I find little joy there now, the ambiance of Yosemite destroyed by wall-to-wall people. There are other regions of the Sierra that have lost their full flavor through the imposition of restrictions designed to protect them. Everywhere the operative phrase is "not allowed", which completely destroys the spirit of the Sierra and offends the memories of everyone schooled in these mountains.

Put simply and directly, the problem is population. Too many are demanding too much, and there is no way to make any more. The tragedy of Lake Tahoe is directly attributable to too much; none of the practices which are now killing the lake and despoiling the surrounding basin were, by themselves, a deadly threat two decades ago. Tahoe could have gone on contending with the waste, noise and commerce indefinitely, and still retained the wonderous qualities that made it the jewel of the Sierra. But too many people demanded a share of the experience, and the effects can never be undone. The recognition of this fact brought the Disney development of Mineral King to a grinding halt. Decades ago, when a resort was first suggested, the Sierra Club was actively involved in the planning, solicitation, and selection of a developer. Disney did not emerge as some ogre, thrusting its will upon an unsuspecting public, but the Club and others involved in the early proposals recognized that any improvement in access would bury Mineral King under an avalanche of people. The apparent bad guys (Disney) were almost innocent bystanders; the good guys (Sierra Club) were partially culpable for initiating the project; and the apparent innocent bystanders (the public) would have been the eventual villains.

There are no easy answers for the future of the Sierra, and indeed there may be no satisfactory answers at all. The mountains offer a great deal to man, but they are really little more than what we make of them, and what they inspire us to find in ourselves. The mountains have been tried and found generous by centuries of man; man is now the one on trial.

Minarets and Ritter Peak surrounded in clouds. Left: Snow melt on rocky soil of Big Pine Canyon.

The 12,264 foot (3,738 meters)
Matterhorn Peak and
The Cleaver are prominent
features of the Sawtooth
Crest above Twin Lakes,
Hoover Wilderness.
Right: Contorted Western
juniper holds a tenacious
footing on Polly Dome
in Yosemite National Park.

Aspen and sage
dotted moraine reflect
in Bishop Park
on the east slope.
Left: Snow melt
patterns change daily
with passing of spring
into summer at
Thousand Island Lake,
Minarets Wilderness.

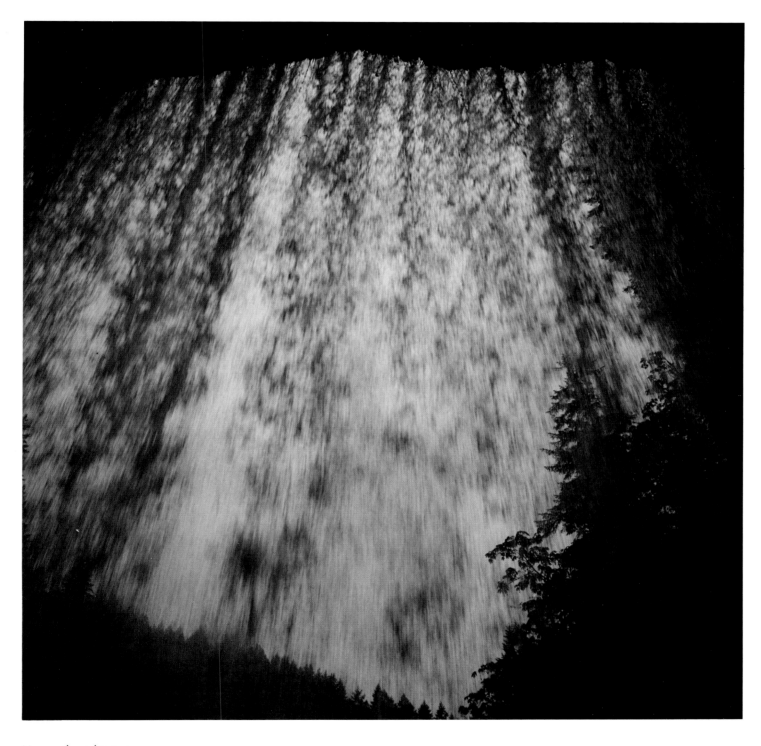

Heavy thunderous
summer cloudburst shears
off ledge above Ediza
Lake. Left: Storm edge
stills the air passing
above a mirror-like pool in
Minarets Wilderness.
Mount Ritter, 13,957 foot
(4,254 meters) and 12,945
foot (3,946 meters)
Banner Peak.

Fragments of symmetrical
basaltic columns lay
tumbled in talus below
standing wall at Devils
Postpile National Monument.
Left: Red Indian paintbrush,
Castilleja miniata,
and yellow yarrow, *Erio
phyllum confertiflorum,*
with sage in Minaret summit.

Peaks of the Ritter
Ridge await a summer
storm viewed from
Minaret summit.
Detail: Water droplet
on blades of grass.
Detail far left:
Color spectrum plays
on spray of Rainbow Falls,
San Joaquin River.

Cloudscape in 12,643 foot
(3,738 meters) Mono Pass
opens new vista into
Mono Creek basin on the
westside. Right: Wind
engravings and deeply
grooved snow cups slow
down the exaltation of
reaching the crest above
Big Pine Canyon,
John Muir Wilderness.

Pioneer Lakes Basin.
The 13,468 foot (4,105 meters)
Mount Mills and 13,715 foot
(4,180 meters) Mount Abbot,
13,713 foot (4,180 meters)
Dade and Bear Creek Spire
cluster above the fourth
recess, John Muir Wilderness.
Left: Red columbine
Aquilegia truncata.

Water ouzel pauses briefly
before bringing food to
young in nest under large
boulder behind. Right:
Rock Creek sings
a roaring spring song below
Mount Abbot,
John Muir Wilderness.
Pages 76 and 77:
Timberline, Pioneer Lakes Basin.

Western juniper in its
exposed rock habitat,
rooted in crevices
and exposed to fierce
winds. Upper Tenaya
Canyon. Detail:
Whitebark trunk. Left:
Upturned whitebark
root system in
Pioneer Lakes Basin.

79

Cumulus reflection
in shallow trailside
pond. South Fork,
Bishop Creek.
Right: A lone delicate
columbine
Aquilegia pubescens
in bloom against
a granite stage
upper Bishop Creek.

Sierra shooting
star *Dodecatheon*
jeffreyi along
shoreline of Palisade
Lake, Kings Canyon
National Park. Left:
Noon reflection of
13,323 foot (4,061 meters)
Mount Thompson
into Blue Lake

Early morning
alpine reflection
Bullfrog Lake,
Kings Canyon
National Park.
Detail: Sierra
Crest image
abstracted through
ice slab in
mid August.

The 12,126 foot
(3,696 meters)
Painted Lady and
upper Rae Lake,
Rae Lakes Basin.
Left: Evening glow,
whitebark stump in
Bullfrog Lake.
Vidette Peaks above
John Muir Trail.

Ladybird beetles
cling together on
branch and grass tips
in the western
foothills where they
feed on aphids.
Left: Evening sunburst
through white fir
overlooking western
slopes of the range.

Whitebark trunk
at turn of a switchback
in Kearsarge Pass,
John Muir Wilderness.
Left: A flickering
glow of sunrise before
an approaching storm
on 13,570 foot (4,136
meters) Mount Brewer,
Kings Canyon National Park.

Upper left: Shooting star. Upper right:
Yellow legged frog. Middle left: Sierra
primrose. Middle right: Bush monkey-
flower. Lower left: Grouse. Lower right:
Pale laurel. Page 93: Basaltic columns,
Devils Postpile National Monument.

Page 94: Timeless flow of
Cascade Creek. Page 95:
Fallen branch in bed of
yellow-throated gillia,
Linanthus montanus. Above:
Rugged 13,632 foot (4,155
meters) University Peak and
Bullfrog Lake. Right: Swarm
of pesky mosquitoes along
the Kearsarge Lakes.

Prostrate whitebark snag
laid bare by the
elements on divide
before 11,693 foot
(3,564 meters) Fin Dome
Kings Canyon Park.
Right: Mature
Western juniper along
Great Western Divide
in Sequoia National Park.

Spectacular covy of
cumulus float eastward
over Rae Lakes in
Kings Canyon National Park.
Left: Tuolumne River
continues the process of
carving away the landscape
in its rush to lower
country. Tuolumne Meadows,
Yosemite National Park.

Design in metamorphic
rock below Muir Pass.
Right: Ridge upon ridge
of cold massive rock
looking south from
Glen Pass, in Kings
Canyon. Pages 104 and
105: Frost fractured
summits of the Palisades
from top of Mount Sill.

Morning silhouettes ridge of
peaks, 13,891 foot (4,234
meters) Mount Agassiz,
13,768 foot (4,196 meters)
Mount Winchell, Thunderbolt
Peak, 14,242 foot (4,341 meters)
North Palisade and
Isocles Peak above Dusy
Basin. Left: Same Palisade
Crest at dusk, Kings
Canyon National Park.

Star of sunrise
and the North Palisade,
Dusy Basin, Kings
Canyon National Park.
Right: Palisade glacier
actively quarries away
rock fragments today
on the Palisades north-
side. Big Pine Canyon,
John Muir Wilderness.

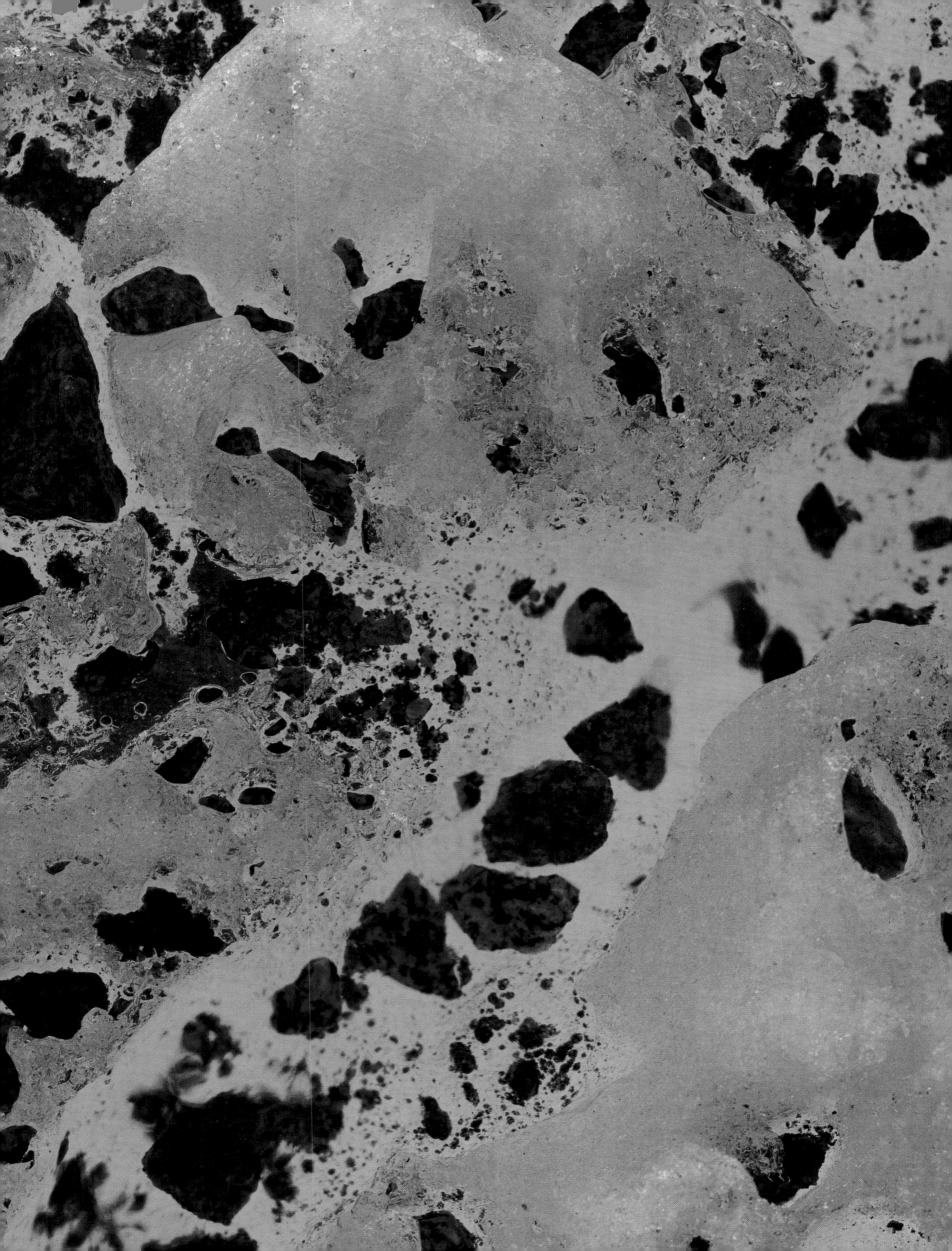

Expanse of rock
desolation sprawls
southward from Mount
Sill along the crest
of the Sierra Nevada to
Mount Whitney. Left:
The Palisade glacier,
an ice age remnant,
inches downhill below
the North Palisade.

Snow plant,
Sarcodes sanguinea
pokes through
forest duff in June
following old snow
drifts. Left: The 12,999
foot (3,962 meters)
Temple Crag etches a
double profile in a
Big Pine Canyon pool.

Sierra primrose
Primula suffrutescens
Left: Fireweed
Epilobium angustifolium
with granite forms
in Little Lakes Basin.
Pages 116 and 117:
The Great Western
Divide from Castle
Rocks in Sequoia Park.

Middle Fork Kaweah River
country from Morro Rock
in Sequoia Park. Left:
Glacial erratic guards the
entrance to valley of the
Yosemite. Page 120: *Sequoia
gigantea,* redwoods in Giant
Forest, Sequoia National
Park. Page 121: Pine and fir,
companions to the sequoias.

Bigelow's sneezeweed
Helenium bigelouii,
and swamp onion,
Allium validum,
upper Hamilton Lakes
Basin. Sequoia
National Park. Left:
Late summer flow of
Hamilton Creek, Middle
Fork Kaweah River.

An alpine cascade
at the base of a sheer
face of Mount Stewart,
Great Western Divide,
along the High Sierra Trail.
Right: A polished
sculpture of
foxtail pine, Cottonwood
Lakes Basin, in the
John Muir Wilderness.

East Fork Kaweah
River in Mineral
King, 12,405 foot (3,781
meters) Florence Peak
and Vandever Mountain
hold Farwell Gap to
the south. Left:
Giant sequoias in
the Parker Grove,
Sequoia National Park.

January moonset over the Sierra Nevada.

ABOUT THE PHOTOGRAPHY

This collection of photographs is for me part of an unending journey...an affair revealing my experience with light, space and time...an unending search for eternal beauty...a continual searching of new horizons and impressions. The photographs are personally significant because they are an important part of the universal "me" in each...an identity in a fast changing world.

Introduction to the Sierra Nevada came early to me (eight years old) with numerous lengthy pack trips bobbing and poking behind my Mother and Father, and at times perched on a stubborn mule. We hiked over legendary passes like Muir, Glen, Forester, Pinchot, Kearsarge, and Kaweah Gap, and had memorable dusty climbs out of canyons like the Kings, Kern and Yosemite. Then catching a beautiful golden or rainbow trout was my inspiration...an inspiration that, in the 1970's slowly evolved into a deepening appreciation not only for those 14 inchers, but their icy lake homes amid stark granite bastions and the streams which trickle down from them.

When working in the field and especially in wild places, I am able to "see" critically. The further back in I hike the greater the challenge and excitement. The eerie, bold, stark and monumental forms—mountains, canyons, valleys, and hills—are what inspire and motivate my directions, both consciously and unconsciously. In most instances I will plan a scheduling of photographs. First to discover and explore a strong location, sizing up its elements, getting a feel for its potential. Later, at a favorable hour of the day or time of the season, I will return and go to work. Much time is spent organizing the events of my personal life to fit into an exciting pattern/sequence of photographing in the field to accommodate both the annual and daily flow of nature.

After some six and a half years at Rochester Institute of Technology in New York and Art Center College of Design in Los Angeles, I have studied under the tutorship of nature, and followed my own intuition and perceptions. When photographing, I tune in to the natural rhythms and pulse of the land...a total embrace with the landscape.

The biggest concern is to communicate and champion the stark beauty that is nature—its wildness, its opposites...a need to relate to a sense of place and time...to an eternal truth. I like to feel my work will lend something toward realizing where we, as humans, are: a honing of our vision, a quickened awareness of the natural world. Making photographic impressions of the mystical forces of nature totally involves me. I have dedicated the rest of my life to this pursuit.

May you walk in beauty.

DAVID MUENCH